I0559286

Walk In God's Grace

31-Day Devotional

MINISTER ALICE JENKINS-CORLEW

www.TrueVinePublishing.org

Walk In God's Grace
Alice Jenkins-Corlew

Published by True Vine Publishing Co.
810 Dominican Dr.
Nashville, TN 37228
www.TrueVinePublishing.org

Copyright © 2024 by Alice Jenkins-Corlew

All rights reserved. No part of this book may be reproduced in any form or by any electronic or mechanical means, including information storage and retrieval or mechanical means without permission in writing from the publisher, except by a reviewer who may quote brief passages in a review.

ISBN: 978-1-962783-92-7 Paperback
ISBN 978-1-962783-42-2eBook

Printed in the United States of America—First printing

Scripture quotations marked KJV are taken from the Holy Bible King James Version

DEDICATION

I would like to dedicate this book to my parents, husband, siblings, children, grandchildren, and my aunt Dorothy Orr. Thank you all for your love and support.

ACKNOWLEDGMENTS

I would like to acknowledge my parents, Harry Jenkins and Alice-Jenkins Harding, for their love and support.

My husband Tyrone for his support and encouragement.

My sister, Elder Janice, for her prayers and godly wisdom; my daughters, Sha and Tosha, for their support when needed; my aunt Dorothy Orr for her love and support; and last but not least, my grandchildren for their listening ears and love.

Special acknowledgment to my spiritual parents, Bishop Horace and Kiwanis Hockett, for teaching me godly principles.

The Grannis Family for their love, encouragement and support throughout the years.

INTRODUCTION

This devotional is to restore you, encourage you, build you up in your faith, and draw you closer to Christ Jesus. What a friend we have in Jesus. He calls us friend. John 15:15 (KJV) states, "But I have called you friends, for all things that I heard from My Father I have made known to you."

1 Peter 5:7 (KJV) says, "Casting all your care upon Him, for He cares for you." As you start reading this devotional, cast all your cares on Jesus. He's your caretaker.

Romans 10:9 (KJV): "If you confess with your mouth the Lord Jesus and believe in your heart that God has raised Him from the dead, you will be saved."

DAY 1

Yesterday Is Gone, Today Is Now, And Tomorrow Is Our Future Walk in grace.

2 Peter 3:18 (KJV): "But grow in grace, and in the knowledge of our Lord and Savior Jesus Christ. To Him be glory both now and forever. Amen."

2 Corinthians 5:21 (KJV): "For He made Him who knew no sin to be sin for us, that we might become the righteousness of God in Him."

_____

_____

_____

_____

_____

_____

DAY 2

Don't give up on your visions. Add to them.

Habakkuk 2:2 (KJV): "Then the Lord answered me and said, 'Write the vision and make it plain on tablets, that he may run who reads it.'"

_____

_____

_____

_____

_____

_____

_____

_____

_____

DAY 3

Listen to God
"No matter how you see it"
God knows how to fix it!

Luke 18:27 (KJV): "But He said, 'The things which are impossible with men are possible with God.'"

_____

_____

_____

_____

_____

_____

_____

_____

DAY 4

Just because it hasn't happened yet, don't stop believing #nowfaith

Hebrews 11:1 (KJV): "Now faith is the substance of things hoped for, the evidence of things not seen."

DAY 5

Don't just tell the dream, live it.

Romans 11:29 (CSB): "Since God's gracious gifts and calling are irrevocable."

_____

_____

_____

_____

_____

_____

_____

_____

_____

_____

_____

DAY 6

Total Praise is always the answer.

Psalm 100:4 (KJV): "Enter into His gates with thanksgiving, and into His courts with praise. Be thankful to Him, and bless His name."

_____

_____

_____

_____

_____

_____

_____

_____

DAY 7

Walk in wisdom and wisdom will walk with you.

Proverbs 3:13-18 (KJV): "Happy is the man that findeth wisdom, and the man that getteth understanding."

_____

_____

_____

_____

_____

_____

_____

_____

_____

DAY 8

Hold on to God. He's still in control!!

Jude 1:25 (KJV): "To God our Savior, who alone is wise, be glory and majesty, dominion and power, both now and forever. Amen."

_____

_____

_____

_____

_____

_____

_____

_____

_____

DAY 9

I see the impossible looking ahead.

Luke 1:37 (KJV): "For with God nothing shall be impossible."

DAY 10

Don't give up. The Holy Spirit is fighting for you.

Exodus 14:14 (KJV): "The Lord shall fight for you, and ye shall hold your peace."

_____

_____

_____

_____

_____

_____

_____

_____

_____

DAY 11

Stop grieving over your past and let God walk you into your future.

Romans 8:18 (KJV): "For I consider that the sufferings of this present time are not worthy to be compared with the glory which shall be revealed in us."

DAY 12

This is a temporary setback for an everlasting setup!!

John 3:16 (KJV): "For God so loved the world that He gave His only begotten Son, that whoever believes in Him should not perish but have everlasting life."

_____

_____

_____

_____

_____

_____

_____

_____

_____

DAY 13

Choose joy for your strength.

Nehemiah 8:10 (KJV): "For the joy of the Lord is your strength."

_____

_____

_____

_____

_____

_____

_____

_____

_____

_____

_____

DAY 14

Position yourself to talk to God.

James 4:8 (NIV): "Come near to God and He will come near to you. Wash your hands, you sinners, and purify your hearts, you double-minded."

_____

_____

_____

_____

_____

DAY 15

It's time for a "Spiritual Transplant"

Ezekiel 36:26 (KJV): "I will give you a new heart and put a new spirit within you; I will take the heart of stone out of your flesh and give you a heart of flesh."

_____

_____

_____

_____

_____

_____

_____

_____

_____

DAY 16

Pray in Faith. What are you asking for in faith?

Mark 11:24 (KJV): "Therefore I say to you, whatever things you ask when you pray, believe that you receive them, and you will have them."

_____

_____

_____

_____

_____

_____

_____

_____

_____

DAY 17

Infinity - what does this mean to you?

Psalm 147:5 (KJV): "Great is our Lord, and mighty in power."

DAY 18

Calvary was for you! How do you feel about Jesus taking on your sins?

Luke 23:33 (KJV): "And when they had come to the place called Calvary, there they crucified Him, and the criminals, one on the right hand and the other on the left."

_____

_____

_____

_____

_____

_____

_____

_____

DAY 19

Love like God does. Who can you show love to today?

1 John 4:11 (NIV): "Dear friends, since God so loved us, we also ought to love one another."

_____

_____

_____

_____

_____

_____

_____

_____

_____

DAY 20

Renewed! Restored! Refreshed!

Psalm 51:10 (NIV): "Create in me a pure heart, O God, and renew a steadfast spirit within me."

Write your own definition.

_____

_____

_____

_____

_____

_____

_____

_____

DAY 21

It's a new day. Don't let the past hold you hostage.

Isaiah 43:18-19 (NIV): "Forget the former things; do not dwell on the past. See, I am doing a new thing! Now it springs up; do you not perceive it? I am making a way in the wilderness and streams in the wasteland."

_____

_____

_____

_____

_____

_____

_____

_____

DAY 22

The Father God is saying if you look through My eyes you will see the truth.

John 14:6 (KJV): "Jesus answered, 'I am the way, the truth, and the life. No one comes to the Father except through Me.'"

_____

_____

_____

_____

_____

_____

_____

_____

DAY 23

God is your Director.
Keep following Him.

Proverbs 3:5-6 (KJV): "Trust in the Lord with all your heart and lean not on your own understanding. In all your ways acknowledge Him, and He shall direct your paths."

_____

_____

_____

_____

_____

_____

_____

_____

DAY 24

Faint not. I come to restore.

Galatians 6:9 (KJV): "And let us not be weary in well-doing: for in due season we shall reap, if we faint not."

How do you need restoring?

_____

_____

_____

_____

_____

_____

_____

_____

DAY 25

Don't ask why? Ask how?

How can I walk in holiness?

1 Peter 1:15-16 (KJV): "But as He who called you is holy, you also be holy in all your conduct, because it is written, 'Be holy, for I am holy.'"

_____

_____

_____

_____

_____

_____

_____

_____

DAY 26

What has God done for you lately?

Everything!

John 3:16 (KJV): "For God so loved the world that He gave His only begotten Son, that whoever believes in Him should not perish but have everlasting life."

_____

_____

_____

_____

_____

_____

_____

_____

DAY 27

Don't focus on the negative. Reach for the positive.

Philippians 4:8 (NIV): "Finally, brothers and sisters, whatever is true, whatever is noble, whatever is right, whatever is pure, whatever is lovely, whatever is admirable—if anything is excellent or praiseworthy—think about such things."

Write 3 positive things in your life.

_____

_____

_____

_____

_____

_____

DAY 28

Promise Keeper

Psalm 145:13 (CSB): "The Lord is faithful in all His words and gracious in all His actions."

_____

_____

_____

_____

_____

_____

_____

_____

_____

DAY 29

Favor is fair because God is good. And God is great!!!

Psalm 84:11 (NIV): "For the Lord God is a sun and shield; the Lord bestows favor and honor; no good thing does He withhold from those whose walk is blameless."

Name some ways God has been good to you.

_____

_____

_____

_____

_____

_____

Purposed for Purpose

Romans 9:17 (KJV): "For the Scripture says to the Pharaoh, 'For this very purpose I have raised you up, that I may show My power in you, and that My name may be declared in all the earth.'"

_____

_____

_____

_____

_____

_____

_____

_____

_____

DAY 31

Singleness is a WORD, not a punishment. Wait on God.

Proverbs 18:22 (KJV): "He who finds a wife finds a good thing and obtains favor from the Lord."

_____

_____

_____

_____

_____

_____

_____

_____

NOTES

NOTES

NOTES

NOTES

NOTES

NOTES

NOTES

NOTES

NOTES

NOTES

NOTES

NOTES

www.ingramcontent.com/pod-product-compliance
Lightning Source LLC
Chambersburg PA
CBHW061326120626
46546CB00007B/2691